Once Upon a Rhyme

also edited by SARA AND STEPHEN CORRIN

THE FABER BOOK OF MODERN FAIRY TALES
STORIES FOR UNDER-FIVES
STORIES FOR FIVE-YEAR-OLDS
STORIES FOR SIX-YEAR-OLDS
STORIES FOR SEVEN-YEAR-OLDS
MORE STORIES FOR SEVEN-YEAR-OLDS
STORIES FOR EIGHT-YEAR-OLDS
STORIES FOR NINE-YEAR-OLDS
STORIES FOR TENS AND OVER
A TIME TO LAUGH Funny Stories for Children (Faber Fanfare paperback)

retold by SARA AND STEPHEN CORRIN
illustrated by Errol Le Cain
MRS. FOX'S WEDDING

Once Upon a Rhyme

101 POEMS FOR YOUNG CHILDREN

edited by
SARA AND STEPHEN CORRIN

illustrated by Jill Bennett

ff
faber and faber

First published in 1982
by Faber and Faber Limited
3 Queen Square London WC1N 3AU
Printed in Great Britain by
Fakenham Press Limited,
Fakenham, Norfolk
All rights reserved

For Tom

British Library Cataloguing in Publication Data

Once upon a rhyme.
1. Children's poetry, English
I. Corrin, Sara   II. Corrin, Stephen
III. Bennett, Jill
821'.008'09282   PZ8.3

ISBN 0–571–11913–1

Contents

5

Puffing Along and Shooting Up

The Train to Glasgow

Here is the train to Glasgow.
Here is the driver,
Mr MacIver,
Who drove the train to Glasgow.
Here is the guard from Donibristle
Who waved his flag and blew his whistle
To tell the driver,
Mr MacIver,
To start the train to Glasgow.

Here is a boy called Donald MacBrain
Who came to the station to catch the train
But saw the guard from Donibristle
Wave his flag and blow his whistle
To tell the driver,
Mr MacIver,
To start the train to Glasgow.

Here is the guard, a kindly man
Who, at the last moment, hauled into the van
That fortunate boy called Donald MacBrain
Who came to the station to catch the train
But saw the guard from Donibristle
Wave his flag and blow his whistle
To tell the driver,
Mr MacIver,
To start the train to Glasgow.

11

Here are hens and here are cocks,
Clucking and crowing inside a box,
In charge of the guard, that kindly man
Who, at the last moment, hauled into the van
That fortunate boy called Donald MacBrain
Who came to the station to catch the train
But saw the guard from Donibristle
Wave his flag and blow his whistle
To tell the driver,
Mr MacIver,
To start the train to Glasgow.

Here is the train. It gave a jolt
Which loosened a catch and loosened a bolt,
And let out the hens and let out the cocks,
Clucking and crowing out of their box,
In charge of the guard, that kindly man
Who, at the last moment, hauled into the van
That fortunate boy called Donald MacBrain
Who came to the station to catch the train
But saw the guard from Donibristle
Wave his flag and blow his whistle
To tell the driver,
Mr MacIver,
To start the train to Glasgow.

The guard chased a hen and, missing it, fell.
The hens were all squawking, the cocks were as well,
And unless you were there you haven't a notion
Of the flurry, the fuss, the noise and commotion
Caused by the train which gave a jolt
And loosened a catch and loosened a bolt
And let out the hens and let out the cocks,
Clucking and crowing out of their box,
In charge of the guard, that kindly man

Who, at the last moment, hauled into the van
That fortunate boy called Donald MacBrain
Who came to the station to catch the train
But saw the guard from Donibristle
Wave his flag and blow his whistle
To tell the driver,
Mr MacIver,
To start the train to Glasgow.

Now Donald was quick and Donald was neat
And Donald was nimble on his feet.
He caught the hens and he caught the cocks
And he put them back in their big box.
The guard was pleased as pleased could be
And invited Donald to come to tea
On Saturday, at Donibristle,
And let him blow his lovely whistle
And said in all his life he'd never
Seen a boy so quick and clever,
And so did the driver,
Mr MacIver
Who drove the train to Glasgow.

WILMA HORSBURGH

13

November the Fifth

And you, big rocket,
 I watch how madly you fly
 Into the smoky sky
 With flaming tail;
 Hear your thin wail.

Catherine wheel
 I see how fiercely you spin
 Round and round on your pin;
 How I admire
 Your circle of fire.

Roman candle,
 I watch how prettily you spark
 Stars in the autumn dark
 Falling like rain
 To shoot up again.

And you, old guy,
 I see how sadly you blaze on
 Till every scrap is gone;
 Burnt into ashes
 Your skeleton crashes.

And so,
 The happy ending of the fun,
 Fireworks over, bonfire done;
 Must wait a year now to remember
 Another fifth of November.

LEONARD CLARK

Building a Skyscraper

They're building a skyscraper
Near our street,
Its height will be nearly
One thousand feet.

It covers completely
A city block.
They drilled its foundation
Through solid rock.

They made its framework
Of great steel beams
With riveted joints
And welded seams.

A swarm of workmen
Strain and strive,
Like busy bees
In a honeyed hive.

Building the skyscraper
Into the air
While crowds of people
Stand and stare.

Higher and higher
The tall towers rise
Like Jacob's ladder
Into the skies.

JAMES S. TIPPETT

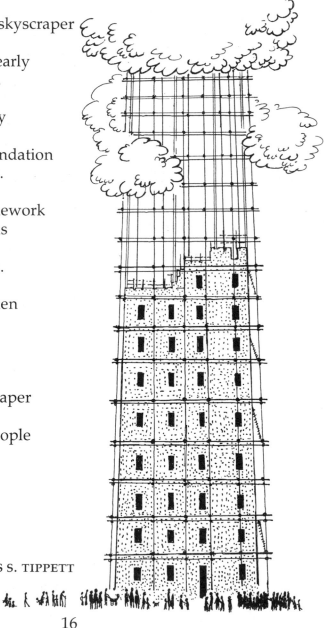

16

Fireworks

They rise like sudden fiery flowers
That burst upon the night,
They fall to earth in burning showers
Of crimson, blue, and white.

Like buds too wonderful to name,
Each miracle unfolds,
And catherine-wheels begin to flame
Like whirling marigolds.

Rockets and Roman candles make
An orchard of the sky,
Whence magic trees their petals shake
Upon each gazing eye.

JAMES REEVES

Soft Landings

Space-man, space-man,
Blasting off the ground
With a wake of flame behind you,
Swifter than passing sound.

Space-man, ace-man,
Shooting through the air,
Twice around the moon and back
Simply because it's there.

Space-man, place-man,
Cruising through the skies
To plant your flags on landscapes
Unknown to human eyes.

Space-man – Race, man,
Scorching back to earth –
To home and friends and everything
That gives your mission worth.

HOWARD SERGEANT

18

Viewpoints

If I Were King

I often wish I were a King,
And then I could do anything.

If only I were King of Spain,
I'd take my hat off in the rain.

If only I were King of France,
I wouldn't brush my hair for aunts.

I think, if I were King of Greece,
I'd push things off the mantelpiece.

If I were King of Norroway,
I'd ask an elephant to stay.

If I were King of Babylon,
I'd leave my button gloves undone.

If I were King of Timbuctoo,
I'd think of lovely things to do.

If I were King of anything,
I'd tell the soldiers, "I'm the King!"

A. A. MILNE

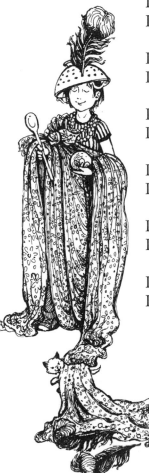

The Blind Men and the Elephant

It was six men of Indostan,
   To learning much inclined,
Who went to see the Elephant
   (Though all of them were blind),
That each by observation
   Might satisfy his mind.

The First approached the Elephant,
   And happening to fall
Against his broad and sturdy side,
   At once began to bawl:
"God bless me! but the Elephant
   Is very like a wall!"

The Second, feeling of the tusk,
   Cried: "Ho! what have we here
So very round and smooth and sharp?
   To me 'tis mighty clear
This wonder of an Elephant
   Is very like a spear!"

The Third approached the animal,
   And, happening to take
The squirming trunk within his hands,
   Thus boldly up and spake:
"I see," quoth he, "the Elephant
   Is very like a snake!"

The Fourth reached out his eager hand,
    And felt about the knee:
"What most this wondrous beast is like
    Is mighty plain," quoth he;
"'Tis clear enough the Elephant
    Is very like a tree!"

The Fifth, who chanced to touch the ear,
    Said: "E'en the blindest man
Can tell what this resembles most;
    Deny the fact who can,
This marvel of an Elephant
    Is very like a fan!"

The Sixth no sooner had begun
    About the beast to grope,
Than, seizing on the swinging tail
    That fell within his scope,
"I see," quoth he, "the Elephant
    Is very like a rope!"

And so these men of Indostan
    Disputed loud and long,
Each in his own opinion
    Exceeding stiff and strong,
Though each was partly in the right
    And all were in the wrong!

                          JOHN GODFREY SAXE

Puppy and I

I met a Man as I went walking:
We got talking,
Man and I.
"Where are you going to, Man?" I said
   (I said to the Man as he went by).
"Down to the village, to get some bread.
   Will you come with me?" "No, not I."

I met a horse as I went walking;
We got talking,
Horse and I.
"Where are you going to, Horse, today?"
   (I said to the Horse as he went by).
"Down to the village to get some hay.
   Will you come with me?" "No, not I."

I met a Woman as I went walking;
We got talking,
Woman and I.
"Where are you going to, Woman, so early?"
   (I said to the Woman as she went by).
"Down to the village to get some barley.
   Will you come with me?" "No, not I."

I met some Rabbits as I went walking;
We got talking,
Rabbits and I.
"Where are you going in your brown fur coats?"
   (I said to the Rabbits as they went by).
"Down to the village to get some oats.
   Will you come with us?" "No, not I."

I met a Puppy as I went walking;
We got talking,
Puppy and I.
"Where are you going this nice fine day?"
   (I said to the Puppy as he went by).
"Up to the hills to roll and play."
   "I'll come with you, Puppy," said I.

A. A. MILNE

I Don't Like You

If I were the Prime Minister of Britain
And you were a snail
I'd be most careful walking round my garden
Not to disturb your trail.

If I were a snail and you were the Prime Minister
It wouldn't be like that.
You'd tramp around in your expensive boots
And squash me flat.

KIT WRIGHT

I asked the Little Boy Who Cannot See

I asked the little boy who cannot see,
"And what is colour like?"
"Why, green," said he,
"Is like the rustle when the wind blows through
The forest; running water, that is blue;
And red is like a trumpet sound; and pink
Is like the smell of roses; and I think
That purple must be like a thunderstorm;
And yellow is like something soft and warm;
And white is a pleasant stillness when you lie
And dream."

ANON.

A Baby Sardine

A baby sardine
Saw her first submarine:
She was scared and watched through a peephole.

"Oh come, come, come,"
Said the sardine's mum,
"It's only a tin full of people."

SPIKE MILLIGAN

The Hippopotamus

Behold the hippopotamus!
We laugh at how he looks to us,
And yet in moments dank and grim
I wonder how we look to him.
Peace, peace, thou hippopotamus!
We really look all right to us,
As you no doubt delight the eye
Of other hippopotami.

OGDEN NASH

27

Horrible Things

"What's the horriblest thing you've seen?"
Said Nell to Jean.

"Some grey-coloured, trodden-on plasticine;
On a plate, a left-over cold baked bean;
A cloakroom-ticket numbered thirteen;
A slice of meat without any lean;
The smile of a spiteful fairy-tale queen;
A thing in the sea like a brown submarine;
A cheese fur-coated in brilliant green;
A bluebottle perched on a piece of sardine."

"What's the horriblest thing *you've* seen?"
Said Jean to Nell.

"Your face, as you tell
Of all the horriblest things you've seen."

ROY FULLER

28

Creatures Great and Small

The Rhinoceros

The rhino is a homely beast,
For human eyes he's not a feast,
But you and I will never know
Why nature chose to make him so.
Farewell, farewell, you old rhinoceros,
I'll stare at something less preposterous.

OGDEN NASH

Mrs. Peck Pigeon

Mrs. Peck Pigeon
Is pecking for bread;
Bob, bob, bob,
Goes her little round head.

Tame as a pussy cat
In the street
Step, step, step,
Go her little red feet.

With her little red feet
And her little round head
Mrs. Peck Pigeon
Goes pecking for bread.

ELEANOR FARJEON

Elephant

It is quite unfair to be
obliged to be so large, so I suppose
you could call me discontented.

Think big, they said, when
I was a little elephant; they
wanted me to get used to it.

It was kind. But it doesn't help if,
inside, you are carefree in small ways,
fond of little amusements.

You are smaller than me, think
how conveniently near the flowers are,
how you can pat the cat by just

halfbending over. You can also
arrange teacups for dolls, play
marbles in the proper season.

I would give anything to be
able to do a tiny, airy, flitting
dance to show how very little a

thing happiness can be really.

ALAN BROWNJOHN

The Butterfly's Ball

Come take up your hats, and away let us haste,
To the Butterfly's Ball, and the Grasshopper's Feast.
The trumpeter Gadfly has summoned the crew,
And the revels are now only waiting for you.

On the smooth-shaven grass by the side of a wood,
Beneath the broad oak which for ages has stood,
See the children of earth and the tenants of air,
For an evening's amusement together repair.

And there came the Beetle, so blind and so black,
Who carried the Emmet, his friend, on his back.
And there came the Gnat, and the Dragonfly too,
And all their relations, green, orange, and blue.

And there came the Moth, with her plumage of down,
And the Hornet, with jacket of yellow and brown;
Who with him the Wasp, his companion, did bring,
But they promised, that evening, to lay by their sting.

Then the sly little Dormouse crept out of his hole,
And led to the feast his blind cousin the Mole.
And the Snail, with his horns peeping out of his shell,
Came, fatigued with the distance, the length of an ell.

A mushroom their table, and on it was laid
A water-dock leaf, which a tablecloth made.
The viands were various, to each of their taste,
And the Bee brought the honey to sweeten the feast.

With steps most majestic the Snail did advance,
And he promised the gazers a minuet to dance;
But they all laughed so loud that he drew in his head,
And went in his own little chamber to bed.

Then, as evening gave way to the shadows of night,
Their watchman, the Glow-worm, came out with his
   light.
So home let us hasten, while yet we can see;
For no watchman is waiting for you and for me.

WILLIAM ROSCOE

36

I Caught a Fish

I caught a little fish one day –
   A baby fish, I think.
It made me jump, I heard it say,
   "I want another drink."
I didn't know a fish could speak –
   That's why I jumped, you see.
It spoke in just a tiny squeak,
   Not loud like you and me.
"You want a drink? You greedy fish,
   "You've had enough, I know.
"I'll put you on my Mummy's dish
   "With salt to make you grow."
"You'd better not," replied the fish,
   "My dad's a great big whale,
"And if you put me on a dish
   "He'll kill you with his tail."
I'm not afraid of whales, I'm not;
   I'd eat one for my tea,
But I was angry with the tot,
   So threw it in the sea.
The little fish was full of joy,
   It gave its head a nod,
"Good-bye," it squeaked," you silly boy,
   "My Daddy's just a cod."

BERTRAM MURRAY

The Fly

How large unto the tiny fly
Must little things appear! –
A rosebud like a featherbed,
Its prickle like a spear;

A dewdrop like a looking-glass,
A hair like golden wire;
The smallest grain of mustard-seed
As fierce as coals of fire;

A loaf of bread, a lofty hill;
A wasp, a cruel leopard;
And specks of salt as bright to see
As lambkins to a shepherd.

WALTER DE LA MARE

The Snail

Snail upon the wall,
Have you got at all
Anything to tell
About your shell?

Only this, my child –
When the wind is wild,
Or when the sun is hot,
It's all I've got.

JOHN DRINKWATER

Ducks

From troubles of the world
I turn to ducks,
Beautiful comical things
Sleeping or curled
Their heads beneath white wings
By water cool,
Or finding curious things
To eat in various mucks
Beneath the pool,
Tails uppermost, or waddling
Sailor-like on the shores
Of ponds, or paddling
– Left! right! – with fanlike feet
Which are steady oars
When they (white galleys) float
Each bird a boat
Rippling at will the sweet
Wide waterway . . .

Yes, ducks are valiant things
On nests of twigs and straws,
And ducks are soothy things
And lovely on the lake
When that the sunlight draws
Thereon their pictures dim
In colours cool.
And when beneath the pool
They dabble, and when they swim
And make their rippling rings,
O ducks are beautiful things!

But ducks are comical things:—
As comical as you.
Quack!
They waddle round, they do.
They eat all sorts of things,
And then they quack.
By barn and stable and stack
They wander at their will,
But if you go too near
They look at you through black
Small topaz-tinted eyes
And wish you ill.
Triangular and clear
They leave their curious track
In mud at the water's edge,
And there amid the sedge
And slime they gobble and peer
Saying "Quack! Quack!". . .

FREDERICK WILLIAM HARVEY

42

Little Trotty Wagtail

Little trotty wagtail, he went in the rain,
And tittering tottering sideways, he near got straight
   again,
He stooped to get a worm, and look'd up to catch a fly,
And then he flew away ere his feathers were dry.

Little trotty wagtail, he waddled in the mud,
And left his little footmarks, trample where he would,
He waddled in the water-pudge, and waggle went his tail,
And chirrup up his wings to dry upon the garden rail.

Little trotty wagtail, you nimble all about,
And in the dimpling water-pudge you waddle in and out,
Your home is nigh at hand, and in the warm pigsty,
So, little Master Wagtail, I'll bid you a good-bye.

JOHN CLARE

43

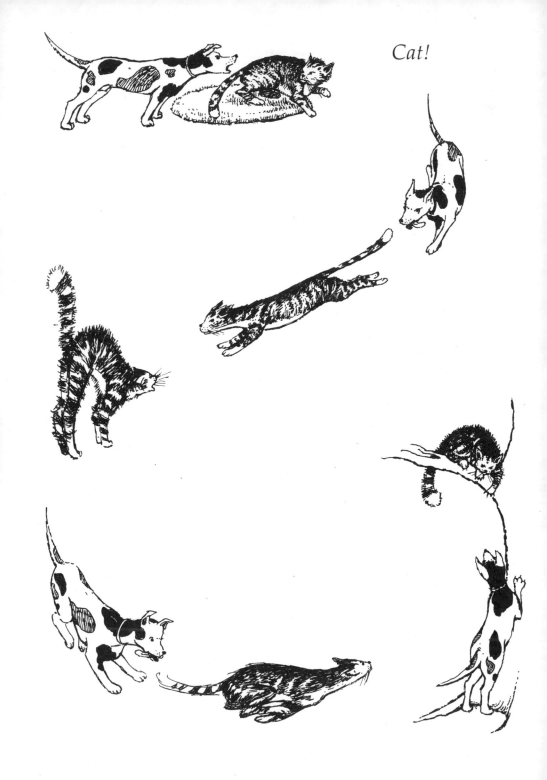

Cat!

Cat!
Scat!
After her, after her,
Sleeky flatterer,
Spitfire chatterer,
Scatter her, scatter her
   Off her mat!
Wuff!
Wuff!
Treat her rough!
Git her, git her,
Whiskery spitter!
Catch her, catch her,
Green-eyed scratcher!
   Slathery
   Slithery
   Hisser,
   Don't miss her!
Run till you're dithery,
   Hithery
   Thithery
     Pftts! pftts!
     How she spits!
       Spitch! Spatch
       Can't she scratch!
       Scritching the bark
         Of the sycamore-tree
         She's reaching her ark
         And's hissing at me
         Pftts! Pftts!
      Wuff! wuff!
        Scat,
        Cat!
        That's
        That!   ELEANOR FARJEON

The Little Hiawatha

Then the little Hiawatha
Learned of every bird its language,
Learned their names and all their secrets;
How they built their nests in Summer,
Where they hid themselves in Winter,
Talked with them whene'er he met them,
Called them "Hiawatha's Chickens".

Of all beasts he learned the language,
Learned their names and all their secrets,
How the beavers built their lodges,
How the squirrels hid their acorns,
How the reindeer ran so swiftly,
Why the rabbit was so timid;
Talked with them whene'er he met them,
Called them "Hiawatha's Brothers".

HENRY WADSWORTH LONGFELLOW
from *The Song of Hiawatha*

The Hen and the Carp

Once, in a roostery,
there lived a speckled hen, and when –
ever she laid an egg this hen
ecstatically cried:
"O progeny miraculous, particular spectaculous,
what a wonderful hen am I!"

Down in a pond nearby
perchance a fat and broody carp
was basking, but her ears were sharp –
she heard Dame Cackle cry:
"O progeny miraculous, particular spectaculous,
what a wonderful hen am I!"

"Ah, Cackle," bubbled she,
"for your single egg, O silly one,
I lay at least a million;
suppose for each I cried:
'O progeny miraculous, particular spectaculous!'
What a hullabaloo there'd be."

IAN SERRAILLIER

Wind and Weather

Something Told the Wild Geese

Something told the wild geese
It was time to go.
Though the fields lay golden
Something whispered – "Snow".
Leaves were green and stirring,
Berries, lustre-glossed,
But beneath warm feathers
Something cautioned – "Frost".

All the sagging orchards
Steamed with amber spice,
But each wild beast stiffened
At remembered ice.
Something told the wild geese
It was time to fly –
Summer sun was on their wings,
Winter in their cry.

RACHEL FIELD

The North Wind Doth Blow

The north wind doth blow,
And we shall have snow,
And what will the robin do then, poor thing?
　He'll sit in a barn,
　And keep himself warm,
And hide his head under his wing, poor thing!

The north wind doth blow,
And we shall have snow,
And what will the swallow do then, poor thing?
　Oh, do you not know
　That he's off long ago
To a country where he'll find spring, poor thing!

The north wind doth blow,
And we shall have snow,
And what will the dormouse do then, poor thing?
　Roll'd up like a ball,
　In his nest snug and small,
He'll sleep till warm weather comes in, poor thing!

The north wind doth blow,
And we shall have snow,
And what will the honey-bee do then, poor thing?
　In his hive he will stay
　Till the cold is away,
And then he'll come out in the spring, poor thing!

The north wind doth blow,
And we shall have snow,
And what will the children do then, poor things?
　When lessons are done,
　They must skip, jump and run,
Until they have made themselves warm, poor things!

ANON.

The Wind

What can be the matter
   With Mr. Wind today?
He calls for me so loudly,
   Through the key-hole, "Come and play."

I'll put my warm red jacket on
   And pull my hat on tight,
He'll never get it off, although
   He tries with all his might.

I'll stand so firm upon my legs,
   I'm strong, what do I care?
Now, Mr. Wind, just come along
   And blow me if you dare.

DOROTHY GRADDON

53

Spring

Spring, the sweet Spring, is the year's pleasant king,
Then blooms each thing, then maids dance in a ring,
Cold doth not sting, the pretty birds do sing –
   Cuckoo, jug-jug, pu-we, to-witta-woo!

The palm and may make country houses gay.
Lambs frisk and play, the shepherds pipe all day,
And we hear aye birds tune this merry lay –
   Cuckoo, jug-jug, pu-we, to-witta-woo!

The fields breathe sweet, the daisies kiss our feet,
Young lovers meet, old wives a-sunning sit,
In every street these tunes our ears do greet –
   Cuckoo, jug-jug, pu-we, to-witta-woo!
     Spring, the sweet Spring!

THOMAS NASHE

A Boy's Song

Where the pools are bright and deep,
Where the grey trout lies asleep,
Up the river and over the lea,
That's the way for Billy and me.

Where the blackbird sings the latest,
Where the hawthorn blooms the sweetest,
Where the nestlings chirp and flee,
That's the way for Billy and me.

Where the mowers mow the cleanest,
Where the hay lies thick and greenest,
There to track the homeward bee,
That's the way for Billy and me.

JAMES HOGG

A Dragonfly

When the heat of the summer
Made drowsy the land,
A dragonfly came
And sat on my hand.

With its blue jointed body,
And wings like spun glass,
It lit on my fingers
As though they were grass.

ELEANOR FARJEON

Ladybird! Ladybird!

Ladybird! Ladybird! Fly away home,
Night is approaching, and sunset is come:
The herons are flown to their trees by the Hall;
Felt, but unseen, the damp dewdrops fall.
This is the close of a still summer day;
Ladybird! Ladybird! haste! fly away!

EMILY BRONTË

Flying

I saw the moon,
One windy night,
Flying so fast –
All silvery white –
Over the sky
Like a toy balloon
Loose from its string –
A runaway moon.
The frosty stars
Went racing past,
Chasing her on
Ever so fast.
Then everyone said,
"It's the clouds that fly,
And the stars and the moon
Stand still in the sky."
But I don't mind –
I saw the moon
Sailing away
Like a toy
Balloon.

J. M. WESTRUP

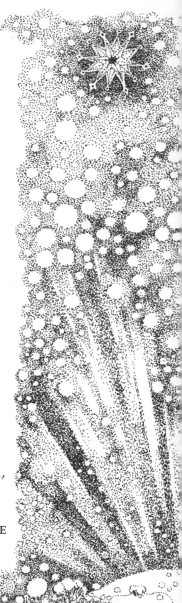

Snow

No breath of wind,
No gleam of sun –
Still the white snow
Whirls softly down –
Twig and bough
And blade and thorn
All in an icy
Quiet, forlorn.
Whispering, rustling,
Through the air,
On sill and stone,
Roof – everywhere,
It heaps its powdery
Crystal flakes,
Of every tree
A mountain makes;
Till pale and faint
At shut of day
Stoops from the West
One wintry ray.
And, feathered in fire,
Where ghosts the moon,
A robin shrills
His lonely tune.

WALTER DE LA MARE

What is Pink?

What is pink? A rose is pink
By the fountain's brink.
What is red? A poppy's red
In its barley bed.
What is blue? The sky is blue
Where the clouds float through.
What is white? A swan is white
Sailing in the light.
What is yellow? Pears are yellow
Rich and ripe and mellow.
What is green? The grass is green,
With small flowers between.
What is violet? Clouds are violet
In the summer twilight.
What is orange? Why, an orange,
Just an orange!

CHRISTINA ROSSETTI

The Intruder

Two-boots in the forest walks,
Pushing through the bracken stalks.
Vanishing like a puff of smoke,
Nimbletail flies up the oak.

Longears helter-skelter shoots
Into his house among the roots.
At work upon the highest bark,
Tapperbill knocks off to hark.

Painted-wings through sun and shade
Flounces off along the glade.
Not a creature lingers by,
When clumping Two-boots comes to pry.

JAMES REEVES

Beech Leaves

In autumn down the beechwood path
  The leaves lie thick upon the ground.
It's there I love to kick my way
  And hear their crisp and crashing sound.

I am a giant, and my steps
  Echo and thunder to the sky.
How the small creatures of the woods
  Must quake and cower as I pass by!

This brave and merry noise I make
  In summer also when I stride
Down to the shining, pebbly sea
  And kick the frothing waves aside.

JAMES REEVES

There are Big Waves

There are big waves and little waves,
Green waves and blue,
Waves you can jump over,
Waves you dive through.

Waves that rise up
Like a great water wall,
Waves that swell softly
And don't break at all.

Waves that can whisper,
Waves that can roar,
And tiny waves that run at you
Running on the shore.

ELEANOR FARJEON

Stocking and Shirt

Stocking and shirt
  Can trip and prance,
Though nobody's in them
  To make them dance.
See how they waltz
  Or minuet,
Watch the petticoat
  Pirouette.
This is the dance
  Of stocking and shirt,
When the wind puts on
  The white lace skirt.
Old clothes and young clothes
  Dance together,
Twirling and whirling
  In the mad March weather.
"Come!" cries the wind,
  To stocking and shirt.
"Away!" cries the wind
  To blouse and skirt.

Then clothes and wind
  All pull together,
Tugging like mad
  In the mad March weather.
Across the garden
  They suddenly fly
And over the far hedge
  High, high, high!
"Stop!" cries the housewife
  But all too late,
Her clothes have passed
  The furthest gate.
They are gone forever
  In the bright blue sky,
And only the handkerchiefs
  Wave good-bye.

JAMES REEVES

The Leaves in a Frolic

The leaves had a wonderful frolic,
    They danced to the wind's loud song,
They whirled, and they floated, and scampered,
    They circled and flew along.

The moon saw the little leaves dancing,
    Each looked like a small brown bird.
The man in the moon smiled and listened,
    And this is the song he heard.

The North Wind is calling, is calling,
    And we must whirl round and round,
And when our dancing is ended
    We'll make a warm quilt for the ground.

                                        ANON.

The Sound of the Wind

The wind has such a rainy sound
Moaning through the town,
The sea has such a windy sound –
Will the ships go down?

The apples in the orchard
Tumble from their tree –
Oh will the ships go down, go down,
In the windy sea?

CHRISTINA ROSSETTI

Check

The Night was creeping on the ground!
She crept, and did not make a sound

Until she reached the tree: And then
She covered it, and stole again

Along the grass beside the wall!
– I heard the rustling of her shawl

As she threw blackness everywhere
Along the sky, the ground, the air,

And in the room where I was hid!
But, no matter what she did

To everything that was without
She could not put my candle out!

So I stared at the Night! And she
Stared back solemnly at me!

JAMES STEPHENS

Odd and Funny

The Sleepy Giant

My age is three hundred and seventy-two,
  And I think, with the deepest regret,
How I used to pick up and voraciously chew
  The dear little boys whom I met.

I've eaten them raw, in their holiday suits;
  I've eaten them curried with rice;
I've eaten them baked, in their jackets and boots,
  And found them exceedingly nice.

But now that my jaws are too weak for such fare,
  I think it exceedingly rude
To do such a thing, when I'm quite well aware
  Little boys do not like to be chewed.

And so I contentedly live upon eels,
  And try to do nothing amiss,
And I pass all the time I can spare from my meals
  In innocent slumber – like this.

CHARLES EDWARD CARRYL

My Sister Jane

And I say nothing – no, not a word
About our Jane. Haven't you heard?
She's a bird, a bird, a bird, a bird.
Oh it never would do to let folks know
My sister's nothing but a great big crow.

Each day (we daren't send her to school)
She pulls on stockings of thick blue wool
To make her pin crow legs look right,
Then fits a wig of curls on tight,
And dark spectacles – a huge pair
To cover her very crowy stare.
Oh it never would do to let folks know
My sister's nothing but a great big crow.

When visitors come she sits upright
(With her wings and her tail tucked out of sight).
They think her queer but extremely polite.
Then when the visitors have gone
She whips out her wings and with her wig on
Whirls through the house at the height of your head –
Duck, duck, or she'll knock you dead.
Oh it never would do to let folks know
My sister's nothing but a great big crow.

At meals whatever she sees she'll stab it –
Because she's a crow and that's a crow's habit.
My mother says "Jane! Your manners! Please!"
Then she'll sit quietly on the cheese,
Or play the piano nicely by dancing on the keys –
Oh it never would do to let folks know
My sister's nothing but a great big crow.

TED HUGHES

Between Birthdays

My birthdays take so long to start.
They come along a year apart.
It's worse than waiting for a bus;
I fear I used to fret and fuss,
But now, when by impatience vexed
Between one birthday and the next,
I think of all that I have seen
That keeps on happening in between.
The songs I've heard, the things I've done,
Make my unbirthdays not so un-

OGDEN NASH

71

Look at all those Monkeys

Look at all those monkeys
Jumping in their cage.
Why don't they all go out to work
And earn a decent wage?

How can you say such silly things,
And you a son of mine?
Imagine monkeys travelling on
The Morden–Edgware line!

But what about the Pekinese!
They have an allocation.
"Don't travel during Peke hour,"
It says on every station.

My Gosh, you're right, my clever boy,
I never thought of that!
And so they left the monkey house,
While an elephant raised his hat.

SPIKE MILLIGAN

Maggie

There was a small maiden named Maggie,
Whose dog was enormous and shaggy;
The front end of him
Looked vicious and grim –
But the tail end was friendly and waggy.

ANON.

Meetings and Absences

How does your little toe
In the bed so long and bare,
Keep on discovering
The top sheet's little tear?

ROY FULLER

The Visitor

John's manners at the table
   Were very sad to see.
You'd scarce believe a child could act
   In such a way as he.

He smacked his lips and gobbled,
   His nose down in his plate.
You might have thought that he was starved,
   So greedily he ate.

He'd snatch for what he wanted,
   And never once say "please",
Or, elbows on the table,
   He'd sit and take his ease.

In vain papa reproved him;
   In vain mamma would say,
"You really ought to be ashamed
   To eat in such a way."

One day when lunch was ready,
    And John came in from play,
His mother said, "A friend has come
    To eat with you today."

"A friend of mine?" cried Johnny,
    "Whoever can it be?"
"He's at the table," mother said,
    "You'd better come and see."

Into the dining room he ran,
    A little pig was there,
It had a napkin round its neck,
    And sat up in a chair.

"This is your friend," his father cried,
    "He's just a pig, it's true
But he might really be your twin,
    He acts so much like you."

"Indeed he's *not* my friend," cried John,
    With red and angry face.
"If he sits there beside my chair
    I'm going to change my place."

"No, no," his father quickly cried,
    "Indeed that will not do.
Sit down at once where you belong,
    He's come to visit *you*."

Now how ashamed was little John;
    But there he had to sit,
And see the piggy served with food,
    And watch him gobble it.

"John," said mamma, "I think your friend
  Would like a piece of bread."
"And pass him the potatoes, too,"
  Papa politely said.

The other children laughed at this,
  But father shook his head.
"Be still, or leave the room at once;
  It's not a joke," he said.

"Oh mother, send the pig away,"
  With tears cried little John.
"I'll never eat that way again,
  If only he'll be gone."

"Why," said mamma, "since that's the case
  And you your ways will mend,
Perhaps we'd better let him go.
  Perhaps he's not your friend."

Now John has learned his lesson,
  For ever since that day
He's lost his piggish manners,
  And eats the proper way.

And papa, and his mother too,
Are both rejoiced to see
How mannerly and how polite
Their little John can be.

KATHERINE PYLE

Toucannery

Whatever one toucan can do
is sooner done by toucans two
and three toucans it's very true
can do much more than two can do

and toucans numbering two plus two can
manage more than all the zoo can
in fact there is no toucan who can
do what four or three or two can.

JACK PRELUTSKY

The Old Man Who Lived in the Woods

There was an old man who lived in the woods
    As you can plainly see,
Who said he could do more work in a day,
    Than his wife could do in three.

"With all my heart," the old woman said,
    "But then you must allow,
That you must do my work for a day,
    And I'll go follow the plough.

"You must milk the tiny cow,
    Lest she should go quite dry,
And you must feed the little pigs
    That live in yonder sty.

"You must watch the speckled hen,
    For fear she lays astray,
And not forget the spool of yarn
    That I spin every day."

The old woman took the staff in her hand,
    And went to follow the plough;
And the old man took the pail on his head
    And went to milk the cow.

But Tiny she winked and Tiny she blinked,
    And Tiny she tossed her nose,
And Tiny she gave him a kick on the shins
    Till the blood ran down his toes.

Then "Whoa, Tiny!" and "So, Tiny!
    My pretty little cow, stand still!
If ever I milk you again," he said,
    "It will be against my will."

And then he went to feed the pigs
  That lived within the sty;
The old sow ran against his legs
  And threw him in the mire.

And then he watched the speckled hen
  Lest she might lay astray;
But he quite forgot the spool of yarn
  That his wife spun every day.

Then the old man swore by the sun and the moon,
  And the green leaves on the tree,
That his wife could do more work in a day
  Than he could do in three.

And when he saw how well she ploughed,
  And ran the furrows even,
He swore she could do more work in a day
  Than he could do in seven.

ANON.

79

Teddy Bear

A bear, however hard he tries,
Grows tubby without exercise.
Our Teddy Bear is short and fat,
Which is not to be wondered at;
He gets what exercise he can
By falling off the ottoman,
But generally seems to lack
The energy to clamber back.

Now tubbiness is just the thing
Which gets a fellow wondering;
And Teddy worried lots about
The fact that he was rather stout.
He thought: "If only I were thin!
But how does anyone begin?"
He thought: "It really isn't fair
To grudge me exercise and air."

For many weeks he pressed in vain
His nose against the window-pane,
And envied those who walked about
Reducing their unwanted stout.
None of the people he could see
"Is quite" (he said) "as fat as me!"
Then with a still more moving sigh,
"I mean" (he said) "as fat as I!"

Now Teddy, as was only right,
Slept in the ottoman at night,
And with him crowded in as well
More animals than I can tell;
Not only these, but books and things,
Such as a kind relation brings –
Old tales of "Once upon a time",
And history retold in rhyme.

One night it happened that he took
A peep at an old picture-book,
Wherein he came across by chance
The picture of a King of France
(A stoutish man) and, down below,
These words: "King Louis So and So,
Nicknamed 'The Handsome!' " There he sat,
And (think of it) the man was fat!

Our bear rejoiced like anything
To read about this famous King,
Nicknamed the "Handsome." There he sat,
And certainly the man was fat.
Nicknamed "The Handsome." Not a doubt
The man was definitely stout.
Why then, a bear (for all his tub)
Might yet be named "The Handsome Cub!"

"Might yet be named." Or did he mean
That years ago he "might have been"?
For now he felt a slight misgiving:
"Is Louis So and So still living?
Fashions in beauty have a way
Of altering from day to day.
Is 'Handsome Louis' with us yet?
Unfortunately I forget."

Next morning (nose to window-pane)
The doubt occurred to him again.
One question hammered in his head:
"Is he alive or is he dead?"
Thus, nose to pane, he pondered; but
The lattice window, loosely shut,
Swung open. With one startled "Oh!"
Our Teddy disappeared below.

There happened to be passing by
A plump man with a twinkling eye,
Who, seeing Teddy in the street,
Raised him politely to his feet,
And murmured kindly in his ear
Soft words of comfort and of cheer:
"Well, well!" "Allow me!" "Not at all."
"Tut-tut! A very nasty fall."

Our Teddy answered not a word;
It's doubtful if he even heard.
Our bear could only look and look:
The stout man in the picture-book!
That "handsome" King – could this be he,
This man of adiposity?
"Impossible," he thought. "But still,
No harm in asking. Yes, I will!"

"Are you," he said, "by any chance
His Majesty the King of France?"
The other answered, "I am that,"
Bowed stiffly, and removed his hat;
Then said, "Excuse me," with an air
"But is it Mr. Edward Bear?"
And Teddy, bending very low,
Replied politely, "Even so!"

They stood beneath the window there,
The King and Mr. Edward Bear,
And, handsome, if a trifle fat,
Talked carelessly of this and that . . .
Then said His Majesty, "Well, well,
I must get on," and rang the bell.
"Your bear, I think," he smiled. "Good-day!"
And turned, and went upon his way.

A bear, however hard he tries,
Grows tubby without exercise.
Our Teddy Bear is short and fat,
Which is not to be wondered at.
But do you think it worries him
To know that he is far from slim?
No, just the other way about –
He's *proud* of being short and stout.

A. A. MILNE

Dad and the Cat and the Tree

This morning a cat got
Stuck in our tree.
Dad said, "Right, just
Leave it to me."

The tree was wobbly,
The tree was tall.
Mum said, "For goodness'
Sake don't fall!"

"Fall?" scoffed Dad,
"A climber like me?
Child's play, this!
You wait and see."

He got out the ladder
From the garden shed.
It slipped. He landed
In the flower bed.

"Never mind," said Dad,
Brushing the dirt
Off his hair and his face
And his trousers and his shirt.

"We'll try Plan B. Stand
Out of the way!"
Mum said, "Don't fall
Again, O.K.?"

"Fall again?" said Dad.
"Funny joke!"
Then he swung himself up
On a branch. It broke.

Dad landed *wallop*
Back on the deck.
Mum said, "Stop it,
You'll break your neck!"

"Rubbish!" said Dad.
"Now we'll try Plan C.
Easy as winking
To a climber like me!"

Then he climbed up high
On the garden wall
Guess what?
He *didn't fall*!

He gave a great leap
And he landed flat
In the crook of the tree-trunk –
Right on the cat!

The cat gave a yell
And sprang to the ground,
Pleased as Punch to be
Safe and sound.

So it's smiling and smirking,
Smug as can be
But poor old Dad's
Still

Stuck
Up
The
Tree!

KIT WRIGHT

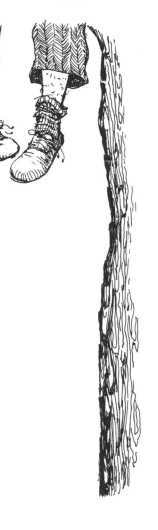

A Thousand Hairy Savages

A thousand hairy savages
Sitting down to lunch
Gobble gobble glup glup
Munch munch munch.

SPIKE MILLIGAN

Mr. Giraffe

O Mister Giraffe, you make me laugh,
You seem to be made all wrong;
Your head is so high up there in the sky
And your neck is so very long
That your dinner and tea, it seems to me,
Have such a long way to go,
And I'm wondering how they manage to know
The way to your tummy below.

GEOFFREY LAPAGE

The Importance of Me

Betty At The Party

"When I was at the party,"
   Said Betty, aged just four,
"A little girl fell off her chair
   Right down upon the floor;
And all the other little girls
   Began to laugh, but me –
I didn't laugh a single bit,"
   Said Betty seriously.

"Why not?" her mother asked her,
   Full of delight to find
That Betty – bless her little heart! –
   Had been so sweetly kind.
"Why didn't you laugh, my darling?
   Or don't you like to tell?"
"I didn't laugh," said Betty,
   "'Cause me it was that fell."

ANON.

89

Miss T

It's a very odd thing –
   As odd can be –
That whatever Miss T. eats
   Turns into Miss T.;
Porridge and apples,
   Mince, muffins and mutton,
Jam, junket, jumbles –
   Not a rap, not a button
It matters; the moment
   They're out of her plate,
Though shared by Miss Butcher
   And sour Mr. Bate;
Tiny and cheerful,
   And neat as can be,
Whatever Miss T. eats
   Turns into Miss T.

WALTER DE LA MARE

The Grasshopper and the Elephant

Way down south where bananas grow,
A grasshopper stepped on an elephant's toe.
The elephant said, with tears in his eyes,
"Pick on somebody your own size."

ANON.

90

The Little Elfman

I met a little elfman once,
    Down where the lilies blow,
I asked him why he was so small,
    And why he didn't grow.

He slightly frowned, and with his eyes
    He looked me through and through –
"I'm just as big for me," said he,
    "As you are big for you!"

JOHN KENDRICK BANGS

91

My Shadow

I have a little shadow that goes in and out with me,
And what can be the use of him is more than I can see.
He is very, very like me from the heels up to the head;
And I see him jump before me, when I jump into my bed.

The funniest thing about him is the way he likes to grow –
Not at all like proper children, which is always very slow;
For he sometimes shoots up taller like an india-rubber
    ball,
And he sometimes gets so little that there's none of him at
    all.

He hasn't got a notion of how children ought to play,
And can only make a fool of me in every sort of way.
He stays so close beside me, he's a coward you can see;
I'd think shame to stick to nursie as that shadow sticks to
    me!

One morning, very early, before the sun was up,
I rose and found the shining dew on every buttercup;
But my lazy little shadow, like an arrant sleepyhead,
Had stayed at home behind me and was fast asleep in
    bed.

ROBERT LOUIS STEVENSON

By the Klondike River

(Spoken by a boy of seven)

Last night, by the Klondike River,
I dug up a fortune in gold!
But I caught a chill in my liver,
Brought on by the bitter cold!

It was far too late to push on,
So I placed the sack on my head;
But gold makes a very hard cushion,
And ice makes a very cold bed.

So I stared at the stars above me,
As my freezing body lay;
And thought of the folk who loved me,
A thousand miles away.

The voice of my dear old mother
Seemed to cry from the icy rocks:
"I told you to wear another
Woolly, and extra socks!"

My body is stiff. I shall die here,
In this lonely Klondike ditch;
And all I can think as I lie here,
Is: Why did I want to be rich?

There's a block of ice on my tummy,
And my frozen toes have curled.
Oh, I'd much rather have my mummy
Than all the gold in the world!

ALAN COREN

Letty's Globe

When Letty had scarce passed her third glad year,
And her young artless words began to flow,
One day we gave the child a colour'd sphere
Of the wide earth, that she might mark and know,
By tint and outline, all its sea and land.
She patted all the world; old empires peep'd
Between her baby fingers; her soft hand
Was welcome at all frontiers. How she leap'd
And laugh'd and prattled in her world-wide bliss;
But when we turn'd her sweet unlearned eye
On our own isle, she raised a joyous cry –
"Oh! yes, I see it, Letty's home is there!"
And while she hid all England with a kiss,
Bright over Europe fell her golden hair.

CHARLES TENNYSON TURNER

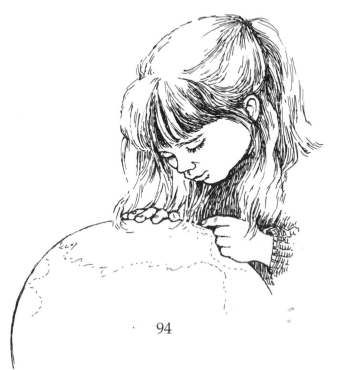

94

In the Mirror

In the mirror
On the wall,
There's a face
I always see;
Round and pink,
And rather small,
Looking back again
At me.

It is very
Rude to stare,
But she never
Thinks of that,
For her eyes are
Always there;
What can she be
Looking at?

ELIZABETH FLEMING

The House I go to in my Dream

The house I go to in my dream
stands beside a little stream
full of dab and minnow and
trout I try to catch by hand
but every single fish is
more elusive than my wishes.

For every time I wish, you see,
I wish that someone else was me.
I stand and wish and call up spells
to turn me into something else
but no matter how I try
I finish up remaining I,
however hard I wish to be
someone else, I am still me.

And so I think that I and you
and every other person, too,
must really be a sort of fish
not to be caught just with a wish.

GEORGE BARKER

96

If You Should Meet . . . Beware . . .

Pirate Don Durk of Dowdee

Ho, for the Pirate Don Durk of Dowdee!
He was as wicked as wicked could be,
But oh, he was perfectly gorgeous to see!
    The Pirate Don Durk of Dowdee.

His conscience, of course, was black as a bat,
But he had a floppety plume on his hat
And when he went walking it jiggled – like that!
    The plume of the Pirate Dowdee.

His coat it was crimson and cut with a slash,
And often as ever he twirled his moustache
Deep down in the ocean the mermaids went splash,
    Because of Don Durk of Dowdee.

Moreover, Dowdee had a purple tattoo,
And stuck in his belt where he buckled it through
Were a dagger, a dirk and a squizzamaroo
    For fierce was the Pirate Dowdee.

So fearful he was he would shoot at a puff,
And always at sea when the weather grew rough
He drank from a bottle and wrote on his cuff,
    Did Pirate Don Durk of Dowdee.

Oh, he had a cutlass that swung at his thigh
And he had a parrot called Pepperkin Pye,
And a zigzaggy scar at the end of his eye
    Had Pirate Don Durk of Dowdee.

He kept in a cavern, this buccaneer bold,
A curious chest that was covered with mould,
And all of his pockets were jingly with gold!
    Oh, jing! went the gold of Dowdee.

His conscience, of course, was crook'd like a squash,
But both of his boots made a slickery slosh,
And he went through the world with a wonderful swash,
    Did Pirate Don Durk of Dowdee.

It's true he was wicked as wicked could be,
His sins they outnumbered a hundred and three,
But oh, he was perfectly gorgeous to see,
    The Pirate Don Durk of Dowdee.

MILDRED MEIGS

Grizzly Bear

If you ever, ever, ever meet a grizzly bear,
You must never, never, never ask him *where*
He is going.
Or *what* he is doing;
For if you ever, ever, dare
To stop a grizzly bear,
You will never meet *another* grizzly bear.

MARY AUSTIN

If You Should Meet a Crocodile . . .

If you should meet a crocodile,
   Don't take a stick and poke him;
Ignore the welcome in his smile,
   Be careful not to stroke him.
For as he sleeps upon the Nile,
   He thinner gets and thinner;
And whene'er you meet a crocodile
   He's ready for his dinner.

ANON.

Mr 'Gator

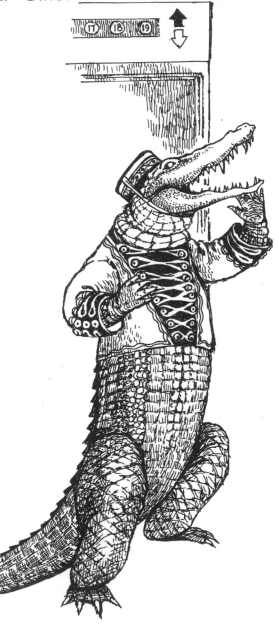

Elevator operator
P. Cornelius Alligator,
When his passengers
were many,
never
ever
passed up
any:
When his passengers
were few,
always managed
to make do.
When they told him:
"Mister 'Gator!
quickly
in your elevator
take us
to the nineteenth floor!"
they were never
seen no more.

N. M. BODECKER

The Spider and the Fly

"Will you walk into my parlour?"
Said the Spider to the Fly;
" 'Tis the prettiest little parlour
That ever you did spy;
The way into my parlour
Is up a winding stair,
And I have many curious things
To show when you are there."
"Oh, no, no," said the little Fly;
"To ask me is in vain;
For who goes up your winding stair
Can ne'er come down again."
"I'm sure you must be weary, dear,
With soaring up so high;
Will you rest upon my little bed?"
Said the Spider to the Fly.
"There are pretty curtains drawn around;
The sheets are fine and thin;
And if you like to rest awhile,
I'll snugly tuck you in!"
"Oh, no, no," said the little Fly;
"For I've often heard it said,
They never, never wake again
Who sleep upon your bed!"

MARY HOWITT

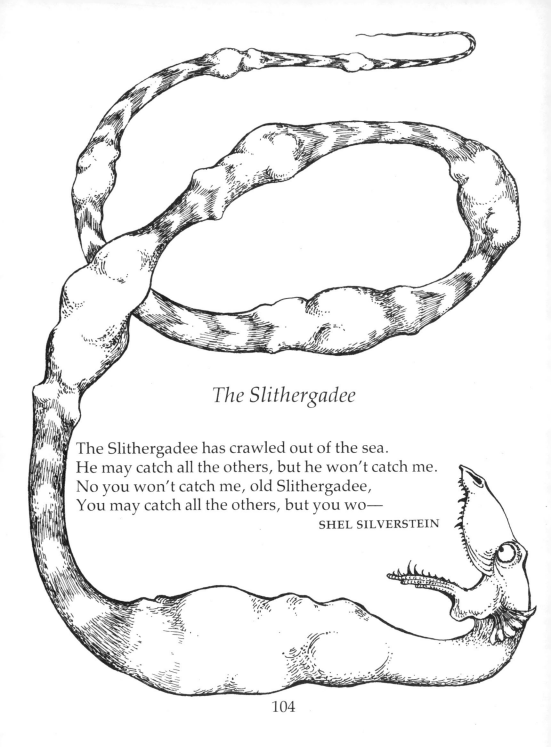

The Slithergadee

The Slithergadee has crawled out of the sea.
He may catch all the others, but he won't catch me.
No you won't catch me, old Slithergadee,
You may catch all the others, but you wo—

SHEL SILVERSTEIN

Isn't it Mysterious?

There was a Naughty Boy

... There was a naughty Boy,
   And a naughty Boy was he,
He ran away to Scotland
   The people for to see –
      There he found
      That the ground
      Was as hard,
      That a yard
      Was as long,
      That a song
      Was as merry,
      That a cherry
      Was as red –
      That lead
      Was as weighty,
      That fourscore
      Was as eighty,
      That a door
      Was as wooden
      As in England –
So he stood in his shoes
   And he wondered,
      He wondered,
He stood in his shoes
   And he wondered.

JOHN KEATS

Danny Murphy

He was as old as old could be,
His little eye could scarcely see,
His mouth was sunken in between
His nose and chin, and he was lean
And twisted up and withered quite,
So that he couldn't walk aright.

His pipe was always going out,
And then he'd have to search about
In all his pockets, and he'd mow
– O, deary me! and musha now! –
And then he'd light his pipe, and then
He'd let it go clean out again.

He couldn't dance or jump or run,
Or ever have a bit of fun
Like me and Susan, when we shout
And jump and throw ourselves about:
– But when he laughed, then you could see
He was as young as young could be!

JAMES STEPHENS

108

My Puppy

It's funny
my puppy
knows just how I feel.

When I'm happy
he's yappy
and squirms like an eel.

When I'm grumpy
he's slumpy
and stays at my heel.

It's funny
my puppy
knows such a great deal.

AILEEN FISHER

A Centipede

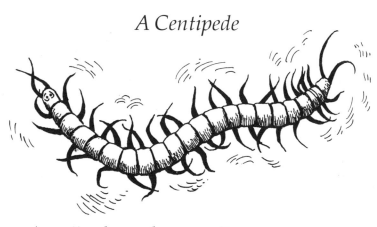

A centipede was happy quite,
Until a frog in fun
Said, "Pray, which leg comes after which?" ·
This raised her mind to such a pitch,
She lay distracted in a ditch
Considering how to run.

ANON.

Macavity: The Mystery Cat

Macavity's a Mystery Cat: he's called the Hidden Paw –
For he's the master criminal who can defy the Law.
He's the bafflement of Scotland Yard, the Flying Squad's
    despair:
For when they reach the scene of crime – *Macavity's not
    there!*

Macavity, Macavity, there's no one like Macavity,
He's broken every human law, he breaks the law of
    gravity.
His powers of levitation would make a fakir stare,
And when you reach the scene of crime, *Macavity's not
    there!*
You may seek him in the basement, you may look up in
    the air –
But I tell you once and once again, Macavity's not there!

Macavity's a ginger cat, he's very tall and thin;
You would know him if you saw him, for his eyes are
    sunken in.
His brow is deeply lined with thought, his head is highly
    domed;
His coat is dusty from neglect, his whiskers are
    uncombed.
He sways his head from side to side, with movements like
    a snake;
And when you think he's fast asleep, he's always wide
    awake.

Macavity, Macavity, there's no one like Macavity,
For he's a fiend in feline shape, a monster of depravity.
You may meet him in a by-street, you may meet him in
    the square –
But when a crime's discovered, then *Macavity's not there!*

He's outwardly respectable. (They say he cheats at cards.)
And his footprints are not found in any file of Scotland
  Yard's.
And when the larder's looted, or the jewel-case is rifled,
Or when the milk is missing, or another Peke's been
  stifled –
Or the greenhouse glass is broken and the trellis past
  repair –
Ay, there's the wonder of the thing! *Macavity's not there!*

And when the Foreign Office find a Treaty's gone astray,
Or the Admiralty lose some plans and drawings by the
  way,
There may be a scrap of paper in the hall or on the stair –
But it's useless to investigate – *Macavity's not there!*

And when the loss has been disclosed, the Secret Service
  say:
"It must have been Macavity!" – but he's a mile away.
You'll be sure to find him resting, or a-licking of his
  thumbs,
Or engaged in doing complicated long division sums.

Macavity, Macavity, there's no one like Macavity,
There never was a Cat of such deceitfulness and suavity.
He always has an alibi, and one or two to spare:
At whatever time the deed took place – MACAVITY WASN'T
  THERE!
And they say that all the cats whose wicked deeds are
  widely known
(I might mention Mungojerrie, I might mention
  Griddlebone)
Are nothing more than agents for the Cat who all the time
Just controls their operations: the Napoleon of Crime!

T. S. ELIOT

The Shadow

When the last of gloaming's gone,
When the world is drowned in Night,
Then swims up the great round Moon,
Washing with her borrowed light
Twig, stone, grass-blade – pin-point bright –
Every tiniest thing in sight.

Then on tiptoe,
Off go I!
To a white-washed
Wall near by.

Where, for secret
Company,
My small shadow
Waits for me.

Still and stark,
Or stirring – *so*,
All I'm doing
He'll do too.

Quieter than
A cat he mocks
My walk, my gestures,
Clothes and locks.

I twist and turn,
I creep, I prowl,
Likewise does he,
The crafty soul,
The Moon for lamp,
And for music, owl.

"*Sst*" I whisper,
"Shadow, come!"
No answer:
He is blind and dumb –
Blind and dumb –
And when I go,
The wall will stand empty,
White as snow.

WALTER DE LA MARE

I Met a Man

As I was going up the stair
I met a man who wasn't there.
He wasn't there again today –
Oh! how I wish he'd go away!

ANON.

The Seed

How does it know,
this little seed,
if it is to grow
to a flower or weed,
if it is to be
a vine or shoot,
or grow into a tree
with a long deep root?
A seed is so small
where do you suppose
it stores up all
of the things it knows?

AILEEN FISHER

Colonel Fazackerley

Colonel Fazackerley Butterworth-Toast
Bought an old castle complete with a ghost,
But someone or other forgot to declare
To Colonel Fazack that the spectre was there.

On the very first evening, while waiting to dine,
The Colonel was taking a fine sherry wine,
When the ghost, with a furious flash and a flare,
Shot out of the chimney and shivered, "Beware!"

Colonel Fazackerley put down his glass
And said, "My dear fellow, that's really first class!
I just can't conceive how you do it at all.
I imagine you're going to a Fancy Dress Ball?"

At this, the dread ghost gave a withering cry.
Said the Colonel (his monocle firm in his eye),
"Now just how you do it I wish I could think.
Do sit down and tell me, and please have a drink."

The ghost in his phosphorous cloak gave a roar
And floated about between ceiling and floor.
He walked through a wall and returned through a pane
And backed up the chimney and came down again.

Said the Colonel, "With laughter I'm feeling quite weak!"
(As trickles of merriment ran down his cheek).
"My house-warming party I hope you won't spurn.
You *must* say you'll come and you'll give us a turn!"

At this, the poor spectre – quite out of his wits –
Proceeded to shake himself almost to bits.
He rattled his chains and he clattered his bones
And he filled the whole castle with mumbles and moans.

But Colonel Fazackerley, just as before,
Was simply delighted and called out, "Encore!"
At which the ghost vanished, his efforts in vain,
And never was seen at the castle again.

"Oh dear, what a pity!" said Colonel Fazack.
"I don't know his name, so I can't call him back."
And then with a smile that was hard to define,
Colonel Fazackerley went in to dine.

CHARLES CAUSLEY

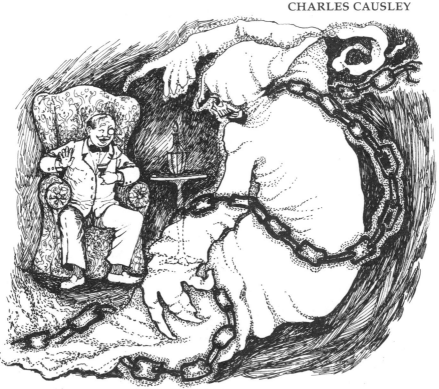

If All the Seas . . .

If all the seas were one sea,
What a great sea that would be!
If all the trees were one tree,
What a great tree that would be!
And if all the axes were one axe,
What a great axe that would be!
And if all the men were one man
What a great man that would be!
And if that great man took the great axe
And cut down that great tree,
And let it fall into the great sea,
What a splish-splash that would be!

ANON.

Sweet Dreams

I wonder as into bed I creep
What it feels like to fall asleep.
I've told myself stories, I've counted sheep,
But I'm always asleep when I fall asleep.
Tonight my eyes I will open keep,
And I'll stay awake till I fall asleep,
Then I'll know what it feels like to fall asleep,
Asleep,
Asleeep,
Asleeeep . . .

OGDEN NASH

Tickle Your Fancy

My Uncle Paul of Pimlico

My Uncle Paul of Pimlico
Has seven cats as white as snow,
Who sit at his enormous feet
And watch him, as a special treat,
Play the piano upside down,
In his delightful dressing-gown;
The firelight leaps, the parlour glows,
And, while the music ebbs and flows,
They smile (while purring the refrains),
At little thoughts that cross their brains.

MERVYN PEAKE

123

The Tickle Rhyme

"Who's that tickling my back?"
    said the wall.
"Me," said a small
Caterpillar. "I'm learning
To crawl."

IAN SERRAILLIER

There was an Old Man from Peru

There was an old man from Peru
Who dreamed he was eating his shoe.
He woke in a fright
In the middle of the night
And found it was perfectly true.

ANON.

I eat my Peas with Honey

I eat my peas with honey,
I've done it all my life,
It makes the peas taste funny,
But it keeps them on my knife.

ANON.

The Habits of the Hippopotamus

The hippopotamus is strong
    And huge of head and broad of bustle;
The limbs on which he rolls along
    Are big with hippopotomuscle.

He does not greatly care for sweets
    Like ice cream, apple pie or custard,
But takes to flavour what he eats
    A little hippopotomustard.

The hippopotamus is true
    To all his principles, and just;
He always tries his best to do
    The things one hippopotomust.

He never rides in trucks or trams,
    In taxicabs or omnibuses,
And so keeps out of traffic jams
    And other hippopotomusses.

ARTHUR GUITERMAN

125

The Quangle Wangle's Hat

On the top of the Crumpetty Tree
   The Quangle Wangle sat,
But his face you could not see,
On account of his Beaver Hat.
For his Hat was a hundred and two feet wide,
With ribbons and bibbons on every side
And bells, and buttons, and loops, and lace,
So that nobody ever could see the face
   Of the Quangle Wangle Quee.

The Quangle Wangle said
   To himself on the Crumpetty Tree:
"Jam; and jelly; and bread;
Are the best of food for me!
But the longer I live on this Crumpetty Tree,
The plainer than ever it seems to me
That very few people come this way,
And that life on the whole is far from gay!"
   Said the Quangle Wangle Quee.

But there came to the Crumpetty Tree,
   Mr and Mrs Canary;
And they said: "Did you ever see
   Any spot so charmingly airy?
May we build a nest on your lovely Hat?
Mr Quangle Wangle, grant us that!
O please let us come and build a nest
Of whatever material suits you best,
   Mr Quangle Wangle Quee!"

And besides, to the Crumpetty Tree
   Came the Stork, the Duck, and the Owl:
The Snail, and the Bumble-Bee,
   The Frog, and the Fimble Fowl;
(The Fimble Fowl, with a Corkscrew leg;)
And all of them said: "We humbly beg,
We may build our homes on your lovely Hat:
Mr Quangle Wangle, grant us that!
   Mr Quangle Wangle Quee!"

And the Golden Grouse came there,
And the Pobble who has no toes,
And the small Olympian bear,
    And the Dong with a luminous nose.
And the Blue Baboon, who played the flute,
And the Orient Calf from the Land of Tute,
And the Attery Squash, and the Bisky Bat,
All came and built on the lovely Hat
    Of the Quangle Wangle Quee.

And the Quangle Wangle said
To himself on the Crumpetty Tree:
"When all these creatures move
    What a wonderful noise there'll be!"
And at night by the light of the Mulberry moon
They danced to the Flute of the Blue Baboon,
On the broad green leaves of the Crumpetty Tree,
And all were as happy as happy could be,
    With the Quangle Wangle Quee.

EDWARD LEAR

Custard the Dragon

Belinda lived in a little white house,
With a little black kitten and a little grey mouse,
And a little yellow dog and a little red wagon,
And a realio, trulio, little pet dragon.

Now the name of the little black kitten was Ink,
And the little grey mouse, she called her Blink,
And the little yellow dog was sharp as Mustard,
But the dragon was a coward, and she called him Custard.

Belinda was as brave as a barrelful of bears,
And Ink and Blink chased lions down the stairs,
Mustard was as brave as a tiger in a rage,
But Custard cried for a nice safe cage.

Custard the dragon had big sharp teeth,
And spikes on top and scales underneath,
Mouth like a fireplace, a chimney for a nose,
And realio, trulio daggers on his toes.

Belinda tickled him, she tickled him unmerciful,
Ink, Blink and Mustard, they rudely called him Percival,
They all sat laughing in the little red wagon
At the realio, trulio, cowardly dragon.

Belinda giggled till she shook the house,
And Blink said *Weeek!* which is giggling for a mouse,
Ink and Mustard rudely asked his age,
When Custard called for a nice safe cage.

Suddenly, suddenly they heard a nasty sound,
And Mustard growled, and they looked all around,
Meowch! cried Ink, and Ooh! cried Belinda,
For there was a pirate, climbing in the winda.

Pistol in his left hand, pistol in his right,
And he held in his teeth a cutlass bright;
His beard was black, one leg was wood.
It was clear that the pirate meant no good.

Belinda paled, and she cried Help! Help!
But Mustard fled with a terrible yelp,
Ink trickled down to the bottom of the household,
And little mouse Blink strategically mouseholed.

But up jumped Custard, snorting like an engine,
Clashed his tail like irons in a dungeon,
With a clatter and a clank and a jangling squirm
He went at the pirate like a robin at a worm.

The pirate gaped at Belinda's dragon,
And gulped some grog from his pocket flagon,
He fired two bullets, but they didn't hit,
And Custard gobbled him, every bit.

Belinda embraced him, Mustard licked him;
No one mourned for his pirate victim.
Ink and Blink in glee did gyrate
Around the dragon that ate the pyrate.

Belinda still lives in her little white house,
With her little black kitten and her little grey mouse,
And her little yellow dog and her little red wagon,
And her realio, trulio, little pet dragon.

Belinda is as brave as a barrelful of bears,
And Ink and Blink chase lions down the stairs,
Mustard is as brave as a tiger in a rage,
But Custard keeps crying for a nice safe cage.

OGDEN NASH

Bengal

There once was a man of Bengal
Who was asked to a fancy dress ball;
He murmured: "I'll risk it
and go as a biscuit . . ."
But a dog ate him up in the hall.

ANON.

There was a Young Lady of Crete

There was a young lady of Crete,
Who was so exceedingly neat,
When she got out of bed
She stood on her head,
To make sure of not soiling her feet.

ANON.

There was an Old Man with a Beard

There was an old Man with a beard,
Who said, "It is just as I feared! –
Two Owls and a Hen, four Larks and a Wren
Have all built their nests in my beard!"

EDWARD LEAR

The Funny Old Man and his Wife

Once upon a time, in a little wee house,
　　Lived a funny old man and his wife;
And he said something funny to make her laugh,
　　Every day of his life.

One day he said such a funny thing,
　　That she shook and screamed with laughter;
But the poor old soul, she couldn't leave off
　　For at least three whole days after.

So laughing with all her might and main,
　　Three days and nights she sat;
And at the end she didn't know a bit
　　What she'd been laughing at.

ANON.

The Ceremonial Band

(To be said out loud by a chorus and solo voices)

The old King of Dorchester,
He had a little orchestra,
And never did you hear such a ceremonial band.
"Tootle-too," said the flute,
"Deed-a-reedle," said the fiddle,
For the fiddles and the flutes were the finest in the land.

The old King of Dorchester
He had a little orchestra,
And never did you hear such a ceremonial band.
"Pump-a-rum," said the drum,
"Tootle-too," said the flute,
"Deed-a-reedle," said the fiddle,
For the fiddles and the flutes were the finest in the land.

The old King of Dorchester,
He had a little orchestra,
And never did you hear such a ceremonial band.
"Pickle-pee," said the fife,
"Pump-a-rum," said the drum,
"Tootle-too," said the flute,
"Deed-a-reedle," said the fiddle,
For the fiddles and the flutes were the finest in the land.

The old King of Dorchester,
He had a little orchestra,
And never did you hear such a ceremonial band.
"Zoomba-zoom," said the bass,
"Pickle-pee," said the fife,
"Pump-a-rum," said the drum,
"Tootle-too," said the flute,
"Deed-a-reedle," said the fiddle,
For the fiddles and the flutes were the finest in the land.

The old King of Dorchester,
He had a little orchestra,
And never did you hear such a ceremonial band.
"Pah-pa-rah," said the trumpet,
"Zoomba-zoom," said the bass,
"Pickle-pee," said the fife,
"Pump-a-rum," said the drum,
"Tootle-too," said the flute,
"Deed-a-reedle," said the fiddle,
For the fiddles and the flutes were the finest in the land,
Oh! the fiddles and the flutes were the finest in the land.

JAMES REEVES

I Saw A Jolly Hunter

I saw a jolly hunter
   With a jolly gun
Walking in the country
   In the jolly sun.

In the jolly meadow
   Sat a jolly hare.
Saw the jolly hunter.
   Took jolly care.

Hunter jolly eager –
   Sight of jolly prey.
Forgot gun pointing
   Wrong jolly way.

Jolly hunter jolly head
   Over heels gone.
Jolly old safety-catch
   Not jolly on.

Bang went the jolly gun.
   Hunter jolly dead.
Jolly hare got clean away.
   Jolly good, I said.

          CHARLES CAUSLEY

The Goat

There was a man, now please take note,
There was a man, who had a goat,
He lov'd that goat, indeed he did,
He lov'd that goat, just like a kid.

One day that goat felt frisk and fine,
Ate three red shirts from off the line.
The man he grabbed him by the back,
And tied him to a railroad track.

But when the train hove into sight,
That goat grew pale and green with fright.
He heaved a sigh, as if in pain,
Coughed up those shirts and flagged the train.

ANON.

The Mad Gardener's Song

. . . He thought he saw a Buffalo
   Upon the chimney-piece:
He looked again, and found it was
   His Sister's Husband's Niece.
"Unless you leave this house," he said,
   "I'll send for the Police!"

He thought he saw a Rattlesnake
   That questioned him in Greek:
He looked again, and found it was
   The Middle of Next Week.
"The one thing I regret," he said,
   "Is that it cannot speak!"

He thought he saw a Banker's Clerk
   Descending from the bus:
He looked again, and found it was
   A Hippopotamus.
"If this should stay to dine," he said,
   "There won't be much for us!"

He thought he saw a Kangaroo
   That worked a coffee-mill:
He looked again, and found it was
   A Vegetable-Pill.
"Were I to swallow this," he said,
   "I should be very ill!"

He thought he saw a Coach-and-Four
    That stood beside his bed:
He looked again, and found it was
    A Bear without a Head.
"Poor thing," he said, "poor silly thing!
    It's waiting to be fed!"

He thought he saw an Albatross
    That fluttered round the lamp:
He looked again, and found it was
    A Penny Postage-Stamp.
"You'd best be getting home," he said,
    "The nights are very damp!"

He thought he saw a Garden-Door
    That opened with a key:
He looked again, and found it was
    A Double Rule of Three.
"And all its mystery," he said,
    "Is clear as day to me!" . . .

LEWIS CARROLL

141

Eletelephony

Once there was an elephant,
Who tried to use the telephant –
No! No! I mean an elephone
Who tried to use the telephone –
(Dear me! I am not certain quite
That even now I've got it right.)

Howe'er it was, he got his trunk
Entangled in the telephunk;
The more he tried to get it free,
The louder buzzed the telephee –
(I fear I'd better drop the song
Of elephop and telephong!)

LAURA E. RICHARDS

The Elephant

The elephant carries a great big trunk;
He never packs it with clothes;
It has no lock and it has no key,
But he takes it wherever he goes.

ANON.

142

Adventures of Isabel

Isabel met an enormous bear;
Isabel, Isabel, didn't care.
The bear was hungry, the bear was ravenous,
The bear's big mouth was cruel and cavernous.
The bear said, Isabel, glad to meet you,
How do, Isabel, now I'll eat you!
Isabel, Isabel, didn't worry;
Isabel didn't scream or scurry.
She washed her hands and she straightened her hair up,
Then Isabel quietly ate the bear up.

Once on a night as black as pitch
Isabel met a wicked old witch.
The witch's face was cross and wrinkled,
The witch's gums with teeth were sprinkled.
Ho, ho, Isabel, the old witch crowed,
I'll turn you into an ugly toad!
Isabel, Isabel, didn't worry;
Isabel didn't scream or scurry,
She showed no rage and she showed no rancour,
But she turned the witch into milk and drank her.

Isabel met a hideous giant,
Isabel continued self-reliant.
The giant was hairy, the giant was horrid,
He had one eye in the middle of his forehead.
Good morning, Isabel, the giant said,
I'll grind your bones to make my bread.
Isabel, Isabel, didn't worry;
Isabel didn't scream or scurry.
She nibbled the zwieback that she always fed off,
And when it was gone, she cut the giant's head off.

Isabel met a troublesome doctor
He punched and poked till he really shocked her.
The doctor's talk was of coughs and chills,
And the doctor's satchel bulged with pills.
The doctor said unto Isabel,
Swallow this, it will make you well.
Isabel, Isabel, didn't worry;
Isabel didn't scream or scurry.
She took those pills from the pill-concoctor,
And Isabel calmly cured the doctor.

OGDEN NASH

If Pigs Could Fly

If pigs could fly, I'd fly a pig
To foreign countries small and big –
   To Italy and Spain,
To Austria, where cowbells ring,
To Germany, where people sing –
   And then come home again.

I'd see the Ganges and the Nile;
I'd visit Madagascar's isle,
   And Persia and Peru.
People would say they'd never seen
So odd, so strange an air-machine
   As that on which I flew.

Why, everyone would raise a shout
To see his trotters and his snout
   Come floating from the sky;
And I would be a famous star
Well known in countries near and far –
   If only pigs could fly!

JAMES REEVES

Piper, pipe that Song again

Piping down the Valleys Wild

Piping down the valleys wild,
Piping songs of pleasant glee,
On a cloud I saw a child,
And he laughing said to me:

"Pipe a song about a Lamb!"
So I piped with merry cheer.
"Piper, pipe that song again;"
So I piped: he wept to hear.

"Drop thy pipe, thy happy pipe;
Sing thy songs of happy cheer;"
So I sang the same again,
While he wept with joy to hear.

"Piper, sit thee down and write
In a book, that all may read."
So he vanished from my sight,
And I plucked a hollow reed,

And I made a rural pen,
And I stained the water clear,
And I wrote my happy songs
Every child may joy to hear.

WILLIAM BLAKE

Acknowledgements

We should like to thank my colleagues Margaret Gross and Margaret Hazelden, Librarians, Children's Books, and Hazel Wilkinson, all of the Hertfordshire College of Higher Education; Mary Junor, Schools Librarian, Barnet; and Veronica Robinson, Senior Children's Librarian, London Borough of Camden, for their invaluable and ever ready help. We should also like to express our gratitude to the librarians at our local Hendon and Golders Green Libraries and to Mary Jean Wilkinson, Headmistress of Milton Bryan School, Bedfordshire, who tried out the poems on children at her school. At every step in the compilation of this book we have relied on the sympathetic guidance and wide knowledge of Phyllis Hunt, Children's Books Editor at Faber and Faber; our gratitude to her is unbounded.

We acknowledge our indebtedness to the following authors, publishers and agents:
A. A. Milne and Methuen Children's Books Ltd. and McClelland and Stewart Ltd. of Toronto for *Puppy and I, If I Were King* and *Teddy Bear* from *When We Were Very Young* by A. A. Milne; A. P. Watt Ltd. and the Estate of Ogden Nash and Little, Brown and Company for *The Rhinoceros*: copyright 1933 by Ogden Nash; first appeared in the *New Yorker*; *The Tale of Custard the Dragon*: copyright 1936 by Ogden Nash; *The Hippopotamus*: copyright 1935 by Ogden Nash: first appeared in the *Saturday Evening Post*, from *Verses from 1929 On* by Ogden Nash; *Sweet Dreams* and *Between Birthdays* from *The New Nutcracker Suite*, copyright 1961, 1962 by Ogden Nash; *The Adventures of Isabel* from *Many Long Years Ago*, copyright 1936 by Ogden Nash; the Literary Trustees of Walter de la Mare and the Society of Authors as their representatives for *Snow*, *The Shadow*, *The Fly* and *Miss T* by Walter de la Mare; *The House I Go To In My Dream* from *To Aylsham Fair* by George Barker, *Macavity: The Mystery Cat* from *Old Possum's Book of Practical Cats* by T. S. Eliot, *My Sister Jane* from *Meet My Folks* by Ted Hughes, all reprinted by permission of Faber and Faber Ltd.; *Mr. 'Gator* from *Let's Marry Said the Cherry and Other Nonsense Poems* by N. M. Bodecker reprinted by permission of Faber and Faber Ltd. and Atheneum Publishers copyright © 1974 by N. M. Bodecker (A Margaret McElderry Book); *Fireworks*, *The Ceremonial Band*, *If Pigs Could Fly*, *The Intruder* from *The Blackbird and the Lilac* by James Reeves, 1952, reprinted by permission of the Oxford University Press; *Stocking and Shirt* and *Beech Leaves* from *The Wandering Moon* by James Reeves, reprinted by permission of Heinemann Ltd.; Michael Joseph for *Mrs. Peck Pigeon*, *Cat*, *There Are Big Waves* and *Dragonfly* from *Silver, Sand and Snow* by Eleanor Farjeon; André Deutsch for *Meetings and Absences* from *Poor Roy* and *Horrible Things* from *Seen Grandpa Lately?* by Roy Fuller; *Look At All Those Monkeys* and *A Thousand Hairy Savages* from *Silly Verse for Kids* by Spike Milligan; *A Baby Sardine* from *A Book of Milliganimals* by Spike Milligan: by permission of Dennis Dobson Books Ltd.; *November The Fifth* by Leonard Clark from

151

152

Index of First Lines

Index of Authors